W9-AOM-154

War Memorials

Arlington National Cemetery

J.S. Burrows

ROURKE PUBLISHING

Vero Beach, Florida 32964

www.rourkepublishing.com

Photo credits: © David Harman: Cover; © Norbert Rehm: Cover; © Robert Dodge: Cover, 5, 6; © TexPhoto: Title Page; Michael Koziarski: Background; © Wikipedia: 7, 18; © john saunders: 8; © David Kaye: 9; © Library of Congress: 10, 11, 13, 14, 17; © Joanna Pecha: 15; © Olga Bogatyrenko: 17; © Terence McArdle: 19; © Nelson Loza: 20; © Associated Press: 21; © juanmonino: 22; © Gary Blakeley: 23; © jim pruitt: 24; © suprun: 25; © Bill Grove: 27; © narvikk: 28

Editor: Kelli Hicks

Cover design by Renee Brady

Interior design by Tara Raymo

Library of Congress Cataloging-in-Publication Data

Burrows, Jennifer.
  Arlington National Cemetery / Jennifer Burrows.
      p. cm. -- (War memorials)
  Includes index.
  ISBN 978-1-60694-425-7
 1. Arlington National Cemetery (Arlington, Va.)--Juvenile literature. 2.
Arlington (Va.)--Buildings, structures, etc.--Juvenile literature. I. Title.
  F234.A7B87 2010
  363.7'509755295--dc22

                                    2009006013

Rourke Publishing
Printed in the United States of America, North Mankato, Minnesota
081810
081710LP-B

www.rourkepublishing.com - rourke@rourkepublishing.com
Post Office Box 643328 Vero Beach, Florida 32964

Table of Contents

Arlington National Cemetery

Arlington National Cemetery is a place where grassy hills and the history of our country meet. This **sacred** burial ground for over 300,000 American heroes is a sea of simple, white marble tombstones on gently rolling hills.

The cemetery is located in Arlington, Virginia, across the Potomac River from Washington, D.C.

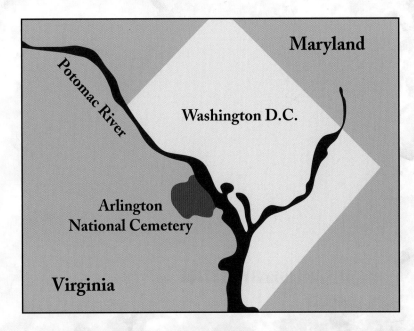

Soldiers from every American war are buried at Arlington
National Cemetery.

5

A national cemetery is a burial ground for **veterans** and members of the armed forces. Presidents, their cabinets, and elected officials can also be buried there.

Calverton National Cemetery

There are 125 national cemeteries in the United States. Arlington is the second largest. The largest is Calverton National Cemetery on Long Island, New York. There are 24 U.S. national cemeteries located in other countries as well.

Arlington provides military honors at its funerals. Soldiers escort the **casket,** gunshots fire into the air, and a **bugler** plays. A burial flag is also available to veterans.

About 2,000 people are buried each year at Arlington. Officials estimate that the cemetery will run out of space by 2030. Three expansion projects will hopefully allow for burials to continue through 2060.

The vehicle used for a military funeral is a wagon called a caisson.

History of Arlington National Cemetery

Several generations of the Custis family, relatives of our first president George Washington, owned the Arlington property before it became a cemetery. They built a mansion called Arlington House on the highest hill and lived there for many years.

Robert E. Lee

A granddaughter of the Custis family married Robert E. Lee, who became general of the Confederate army. Today, Arlington House is a memorial to Robert E. Lee, called the Custis-Lee Mansion.

11

When the Civil War started, the Custis family fled from their home because they feared an invasion by the Union army. Very soon after the family left, the **Union** army set up camp on the property.

The Union government didn't want the Custis family to return to Arlington as the rightful owners. The government created a property tax that required payment in person. When no Custis family members came to pay, the Union government **auctioned** off the property. The Union purchased the house and land for themselves at the auction one year after the Custis family left.

A man named George Hadfield designed Arlington House. Slaves
used concrete, made to look like marble, to build the house.

13

In 1863, soon after the **onset** of the Civil War, a village for freed slaves was established at Arlington called Freedman's Village. The freed slaves received housing, an education, and medical care. The village existed for over 30 years.

   As the Civil War raged, the Union needed a national
cemetery to bury the soldiers who died. The government made
the decision to use the Arlington property as a burial ground.
Private William Christman was the first soldier to be buried
there. Many other Civil War veterans followed.

Years after the Civil War ended, a great-great grandson of the Custis family sued the United States government for illegally auctioning and buying Arlington. His name was George Washington Custis Lee.

After a five year battle, the Supreme Court returned the property to Mr. Custis Lee. The thousands of Civil War dead could not be removed though. In 1883, Congress legally bought the Arlington property from Mr. Custis Lee.

George Washington
Custis Lee

The United States government paid Mr. Custis Lee $150,000 for the Arlington property.

Monuments and Memorials at Arlington National Cemetery

The Arlington National Cemetery proudly displays a variety of monuments and memorials to commemorate military actions and people. The monuments come in all shapes and sizes and remind us of significant events in American history.

The battleship, *USS Maine*, sunk off the coast of Cuba in 1898. A **monument** is dedicated to its 260 crew members at Arlington.

USS Maine Memorial dedicated February 15, 1915

18

Marine Corps Memorial
dedicated November 10, 1954

The Marine Corps **Memorial** is a bronze statue of five Marines and one Navy Corpsman raising an American flag. The statue looks like a photograph taken during a battle in World War II.

19

President John F. Kennedy gravesite completed July 20, 1967

In 1963, President John F. Kennedy died from a gunshot wound. He is buried at Arlington. An **eternal** flame burns at his memorial.

Space Shuttle Challenger Memorial dedicated March 21, 1987

On January 28, 1986, seven crew members died aboard the space shuttle *Challenger*. A monument made of bronze and **granite** honors their service.

The Memorial Amphitheater

The Memorial **Amphitheater** is a stadium made of white marble. It seats 5,000 people. Since 1920, the Amphitheater is where the United States holds its official ceremonies to honor our nation's service members.

The names of the 44 battles fought by American soldiers are inscribed on the sides of the stage of the Amphitheater.

The Tomb of the Unknowns

On the **terrace** of the Amphitheater is the Tomb of the Unknowns. This is one of the most visited sites at Arlington National Cemetery. There is an **unidentified** soldier buried there from World War I, World War II, and the Korean War.

The United States buried an unknown soldier from the Vietnam War at Arlington in 1984. In 1998, Department of Defense scientists used DNA testing to identify the remains as Air Force First Lieutenant Michael Joseph Blassie. His family claimed his body and the tomb remains empty.

The Third United States Infantry

In 1937, the Third United States Infantry Regiment, also known as the Old Guard, started guarding the Tomb of the Unknowns every minute of every day.

The soldiers take turns guarding the tomb. They hold a ceremony each time they switch guards. During the ceremony a relief commander instructs any people present to stand and remain silent. After a thorough inspection of the incoming soldier's uniform and rifle, the guard on duty is relieved and the new guard takes his place at the tomb. Many people gather to watch the changing of the guards at the Tomb of the Unknowns.

Members of the Old Guard participate in 6,000 ceremonies each year.

27

Our nation's heroes are laid to rest with honor and dignity at Arlington National Cemetery. A well maintained landscape and 17,000 trees surround their graves. Many visitors think that Arlington is a stunning place to visit. The largest crowds come on Memorial Day and Veterans Day, but any day is a special day to visit Arlington National Cemetery.

Timeline

1861	The Civil War begins.
1861	The Custis family flees the Arlington property.
1861	The Union Army sets up camp at Arlington.
1862	The Union government auctions off and buys the Arlington property.
1863	Freedman's Village opens.
1864	Arlington becomes a military cemetery.
1883	Congress legally buys the Arlington property.
1920	The Amphitheater is dedicated.
1921	An unknown soldier from World War I is buried at Arlington.
1958	Unknown soldiers from World War II and the Korean War are buried at Arlington.
1984	An unknown soldier from the Vietnam War is buried at Arlington.
1998	Department of Defense scientists identify the unknown soldier from the Vietnam War.

Glossary

amphitheater (AM-fi-thee-uh-tur): a large open-air stadium

auctioned (AWK-shuhnd): sold to the person who offered the most money

bugler (BYOO-guhl-ur): a person that plays an instrument similar to a trumpet but without keys

casket (KASS-kit): a large box a dead person is placed into for burial

eternal (i-TUR-nuhl): lasting forever

granite (GRAN-it): a type of rock

memorial (muh-MOR-ee-uhl): something built to help people remember a person or an event

monument (MON-yuh-muhnt): something to remind people of a person or an event

onset (ON-set): the beginning

sacred (SAY-krid): very important or deserving great respect

terrace (TER-iss): a paved patio space

unidentified (uhn-eye-DEN-tuh-fide): not recognized

Union (YOON-yuhn): the northern states that remained loyal to the federal government during the Civil War

veterans (VET-ur-uhns): people who serve in the armed forces, especially during a war

Websites

www.arlingtoncemetery.net

www.cem.va.gov/cem/cems_nmc.asp

xroads.virginia.edu/~cap/ARLINGTON/arlington.html

www.dc.about.com/od/monuments/p/ArlingtonCemetery.htm

www.findgrave.com

bensguide.gpo.gov/3-5/symbols

31

Index

About the Author

J. S. Burrows is a former teacher who loves writing stories for children. She is deeply patriotic and thinks the men and women who serve in the military are heroes. When she's not writing, she enjoys cooking and playing Dance Dance Revolution with her three kids.